CHA

D0904681

ESSENTIAL
MARINE KNOTS

CHAPMAN

ESSENTIAL MARINE KNOTS

Dominique Le Brun

HEARST BOOKS
A Division of Sterling Publishing Co., Inc.
New York

Copyright © 2004 by Sterling Publishing Co., Inc.
All rights reserved. The written instructions and photographs in this volume are intended for the personal
use of the reader and may be reproduced for that purpose only. Any other use, especially commercial use,
is forbidden under law without the written permission of the copyright holder.

Every effort has been made to ensure that all the information in this book is accurate. However, due to dif-
fering conditions, tools, and individual skills, the publisher cannot be responsible for any injuries, losses,
and other damages that may result from the use of the information in this book.

Original French language edition copyright © 2001 by Tana Éditions
ILLUSTRATIONS BY THIERRY DELÉTRAZ
PHOTOGRAPHY BY MATTHIEU PRIER
MANAGING EDITOR: JULIE ROCHETTE
GRAPHIC ARTIST: YANNICK LE BOURG
LAYOUT: JACQUELINE LEYMARIE

Library of Congress Cataloging-in-Publication Data
Le Brun, Dominique
    [Tous les noeuds marins. English]
    Chapman essential marine knots / by Dominique le Brun.
        p. cm.
Translation of Tous les noeuds marins.
Includes bibliographical references.
    ISBN 1-58816-277-X
    I. Title.
    VM533.L43 2003
    623.88'82--dc21
                                            2003005323

10 9 8 7 6 5 4 3 2 1

Published by Hearst Books
A Division of Sterling Publishing Co., Inc.
387 Park Avenue South, New York, NY 10016

CHAPMAN and CHAPMAN PILOTING and Hearst Books are trademarks owned by
Hearst Communications, Inc.

Distributed in Canada by Sterling Publishing
c/o Canadian Manda Group, One Atlantic Avenue, Suite 105
Toronto, Ontario, Canada M6K 3E7

Distributed in Great Britain by Chrysalis Books
64 Brewery Road, London N7 9NT. England

Distributed in Australia by Capricorn Link (Australia) Pty. Ltd.
P.O. Box 704, Windsor, NSW 2756 Australia

Printed in China

ISBN 1-58816-277-X

ACKNOWLEDGMENTS

We thank Miss Sonia Desjardins (Musée des Terre-Neuvas et de la Pêche), Misters Hubert Berti and Dominique Trépeau, as well as Éditions Gallimard for their invaluable contributions.

CREDITS FOR PHOTOGRAPHS AND ILLUSTRATIONS

Artephot/A. Held: p. 4; Artephot/Oronoz: p. 8; DPPI: p. 26; Fécamp/musée des Terre-Neuvas et de la Pêche/cliché Imagery: p. 5; Musée de la Marine, Paris/Cl. P. Dantec: p. 12 (top); Matthieu Prier: covers and back covers of box and booklet, pp. 16–17, 27, 28; Omega/Ancre: pp. 3 (background), 14, 15, 20, 21, 23, 24, 25, 30 (background), 31 (background); Roger-Viollet: pp. 18, 22; See and Sea/Annie Fyot: p. 12 (bottom).

CONTENTS

PREFACE

How fascinating the spectacle of a boat arriving at a quay, when a sailor jumps down holding a rope and, in one movement, ties a perfect knot, without even looking at what he is doing. There is something magical in the universe of ropes.

Moreover, as Jacques Perret wrote in his amazing *Rôle de plaisance**: "The art of knots is one of the oldest wonders of human industry. The first three tools were the rock, the club, and the rope in the form of vines or straps. But what use would a rope be if we could not tie it? And if you retort with the example of fakirs, who can throw an apparently free rope, keep it totally undone, and heave it up reasonably well, I would reply that, as far as seafaring is concerned, I am reluctant to invoke a reference to fakirs; the education I received does not entitle me to exempt any rope from universal gravitation, and I believe that in the very evening of the day when rope was invented, the knot was discovered, probably a half hitch. In our civilization, the half hitch and the reef knot have rendered as much service as the lever of Archimedes, and by now certainly more than the steam engine or welding."

---

*Jacques Perret, *Rôle de plaisance*, Paris, Éditions Gallimard, 1957.

8

However, whether you agree with our writer or not, all individuals who know knot making are considered sorcerers in their circles. They are those who elegantly solve a problem insoluble for all others. For instance, instantly patching up a broken shoelace (by means of a sheet bend). Every morning, you make a necktie knot, but do you know that it is none other than the bowline used by sailors? Are you a bit of a sorcerer already?

D.L.B.

Rope: A Key Tool
in Human History

When we ask an archae-
ologist how men in
prehistoric times were able to
transport and raise stones
weighing several dozen tons,
the answer is immediate. "As
soon as rope was invented, everything became possible, if one consid-
ers that at that time, the necessary time and manpower did not
have any importance at all." It is known that, since the Neolithic
age, men knew how to plait fibers of flax, hemp, nettle, etc.
They had known for an even longer time how to use flexible
roots and the vines of certain trees. And they also knew how
to cut the skins of animals in a spiral to make strips, as well
as how to recycle the tendons to make thin, strong ropes.

TOP:
A drakkar
handles well at
sea because part
of its frame is
assembled with
flexible cords.

LEFT:
This bas-relief of
the Eighteenth
Dynasty shows
that Egyptian
boats could
transport loads
as heavy as
obelisks.

At the Root of All Technology: The Cord

With the invention of rope, human beings found a means of
uniting the strength of many individuals to move a heavy
object. Undoubtedly, hundreds of people relied on rudimentary
ropes in order to put up huge megaliths, build Egyptian pyra-
mids and Incan temples. In a less impressive area, can one
imagine the progress achieved on the day human beings, for the
first time, sewed animal skins to fit their bodies? The day on
which they tied a stone ax to a handle, which would allow
them to hit with more strength and precision? And, back to the
world of navigation, when they tied many trunks or bundles of
wood together and obtained a platform able to carry a load?
The very first mode of transportation was born.

11

One Thousand Years B.C.: The Inflatable Boat

Two types of boat other than the wooden raft, also appeared very early: skin boats, made of animal skins sewn and inflated to serve as floats for platforms (as we see with the Assyrians, 1000 B.C.); and the kayaks of the Eskimo or Inuit, made of animal skins sewn together over a wooden frame, which date back to 2000 B.C. Even more than with rafts, these inventions were possible thanks to the know-how of these societies: first, in manufacturing strong cords and ropes, and then in using the latter in knot making. Their techniques still astonish us.

BELOW: Evolution of the dugout raft: a hull made of bundles of tied rushes as it was developed in Egypt as well as in South America.

Given what is known in modern technology, we would be tempted to consider frameworks made with strings and knots inferior to those made later with pegs and nails. Concerning navigation, nothing could be less obvious. In fact, it has been a long time since official history has considered the American continent to have been discovered in 1492 by Christopher Columbus's caravels, ships built using the same technique employed in the fabrication of present-day wooden boats. Now, we know that the first "Europeans" to land on the New World were either Irish monks in the sixth century or Vikings in the tenth century. The former navigated aboard currachs, boats made of skins sewn on a framework of oak and wicker, whose assembly was knotted

RIGHT: The drakkar, with its dragon at the prow, has a characteristic silhouette.

together. As for the hulls of Viking drakkars, a major part of the structure was made by lashing. In these two cases, as reconstructions have proven, we know that it is the flexibility thus obtained that gives the hulls their remarkable strength at sea. We also know the fantastic voyages made by the Polynesians across the Pacific aboard dugout canoes with outriggers, whose assembly with ropework was extraordinarily sophisticated.

Today, navigation is the only domain where the use of ropes remains fundamental. And not only for sailing boats. From towing, to tying up to a dock, to pulling a trawl, we continue to use cables and ropes as we have for centuries. The only difference is that stainless steel has replaced untreated metal, and since the 1950s synthetic materials have consigned the vegetable fibers employed since prehistoric times to the scrap heap. But the principle of making rope remains the same.

The North American and Greenland Inuit's kayak appears as a wonder of technology, an admirable boat whose secret lies in the mastery of lashing and sewing. Thus, the elements of the frame are assembled by clever hide or tendon lashing, which prevents the boat from "warping" under the effect of severe changes in weather (important in far northern latitudes).

The Native American canoe, assembled exclusively by sewing and lashing.

13

BRAZA DE LA MAYOR

BRAZA DEL TRINQUETE

AMANTILLO

Galeon del siglo XVII.

The Era of the Wooden Sailing Vessels

Seventeenth-century vessels, such as the galleon on the opposite page, were true cathedrals of wood, rope, and sail. We realize this when we see the *Batavia*, a modern replica of a Dutch East India Company ship that was wrecked on June 4, 1629. Such ships can be described as floating fortified castles. They were designed to brave the dangerous seas of the Indian Ocean and bring back to Holland spices, which were traded for a small fortune. To transport such wealth, nothing was too beautiful, nothing could seem too solid.

The Extraordinary Galleons

On a hull 190 feet long and 56 feet high (the height of a five-story building), the mainmast reaches a height of 174 feet (the height of a cathedral tower). These ships featured three masts on which 1,403 square yards of sail were unfurled (on the *Batavia*), and rigging of hempen ropes held all this in the air. Stainless-steel cables were introduced centuries later, and then only to anchor ships. Thus, apart from metal used for hull nails, chain plates, metal reinforcements, and rudder connections, everything on a ship of that time was made of vegetable material: oak for the hull, pine for the masts, linen for the sails, hemp for the rigging.

Is it at all surprising that to maneuver—and defend—such giants, a crew of a few hundred people was

LEFT AND BELOW: From the seventeenth century to the eighteenth century, we moved from the powerful but clumsy galleon to the much sleeker brig, which carried significantly less cargo.

needed? The *Couronne*, a French vessel that was a contemporary of the *Batavia*, was just 164 feet long, but its mainmast reached 236 feet (the towers of Notre Dame Cathedral in Paris are 226 feet high). The *Batavia* could take 520 men onboard: 40 sailors turned each capstan, and the smallest maneuver required the dispatch of about a hundred topmen to the rigging. Hence the following problem: all these people, as well as the food and water necessary for trips that would last several months without stopovers, took up considerable space. This space would certainly have been more profitable if employed for freight. It is to this concern with profitability that we owe the evolution of rigging: it reduced the number of necessary crew members.

As Jonathan Brunnel reports in *"Berta of Ibiza," Merchant Sailing Ship*, nothing is worse than a rainy day at a Mediterranean port on board a three-masted vessel rigged with vegetable fiber ropes. "I am on watch and a storm is brewing. Disaster! Quickly, I go around the halyards turned on their belaying pins to let them out a bit because, under the effect of humidity, these dried out riggings would become considerably tighter and would surely snap!"

In the Time of Clippers

To this end, the number of sails was multiplied to reduce the surface of each. Consequently, the rigging required less effort and was made considerably lighter. Better yet, it was possible to "set more canvas" with less work. Thus, at the end of the nineteenth century, tea clippers such as the *Cutty Sark* were not much longer than the large galleons. However, the *Cutty Sark* carried 3,600 square yards of sail, two-and-a-half times more than the *Batavia*, but its crew was composed of only about 20 men.

The lightness and simplicity of rigging on three- and four-masted ships at the moment of the invention of the steamboat are truly amazing in relation to the complex mass of a galleon.

The *Cutty Sark* was carefully preserved, and it can be visited today in a dry dock near London, which allows us to admire the perfection of its hull; it is both sleeker for the sake of performance and square for carrying heavy loads. As for the finishing touches in its accommodations, the quality of its fittings, and the exactness of its rigging, we would believe ourselves to be aboard the yacht of a millionaire and not on a simple cargo ship. No expense was spared on those ships that met the increasing demand for fresh Chinese tea. The sooner the vessel arrived at the market, the higher the price its tea fetched. Certainly, the art of riggers reached its height in the seventeenth and eighteenth centuries. Since it was only hemp, whose strength in holding up huge columns of sail is limited, everything was designed to distribute and absorb strain. This is the reason for stays that were larger than the torso of the strongest sailor onboard but which could be badly damaged by a well-placed cannonball during a naval battle.

The saga of three-masted Cape Horners: at that time, entire watches of topmen would rush for the rigging to shorten sail.

The Royal Rope Factory
of Rochefort

S et up under Louis XIV, the arsenal of Rochefort is situated along the Charente River more than 12 miles from the sea. Strange? This location had the enormous advantage of protecting the premises against an attack by the English fleet. After all, the port of Rochefort had a factory with the best strategic interest, rope making, which supplied not only the Royal Navy but also the colonies in America. Given that on a 1,000-ton vessel there were about 50 tons of rope, that a fleet had several hundred vessels, and that even a small battle could extensively damage riggings, one can imagine the activity at the Royal Rope Factory between the seventeenth and eighteenth centuries.

LEFT:
The Royal Rope Factory of Rochefort depicted by Joseph Vernet (1762), and the modern workshop where the rigging of the *Batavia* was put together.

A Palace for Rope

The visitor marvels at the building begun in 1666: it is 1,220 feet long by only 26 feet wide. The single-story building topped by attic rooms is well lit by huge windows. It is of a magnificent simplicity, with the central part being 984 feet long, reinforced at the ends by two larger pavilions. In the middle of the central part there is a detached third pavilion. However, the most astounding thing lies neither in the dimensions nor in the design of the buildings. The wonder of this construction is invisible. It was necessary to build the Royal Rope Factory on a muddy—and therefore unstable—subsoil. Its architect, François Blondel, decided to design a sort of giant

ABOVE:
An ox-drawn cart delivers a load of hemp at the Royal Rope Factory of Rochefort.

raft, a grid of beams to stabilize the soil. This foundation required 18,900 cubic yards of old oak!

The rope factory, set back slightly from the Charente River, marked out the heart of the arsenal. Its north pavilion sheltered the tar warehouse, the south pavilion was the sail loft (nearly 3,000 square yards of sail were needed for a vessel of 1,000 tons!), and the central pavilion accommodated the tar works and the steaming room.

The pulley is the essential complement for rope. From its crudest form, when constructed of a simple hardwood block with a hole—such as a fairlead or a bull's-eye truck—it becomes a very complex object that includes several sheaves, possibly of different diameters, and accessories such as a swivel and a becket. The richness of vocabulary necessary to describe it shows its sophistication.

Ropes of Standard Length

Barges delivered hemp from Auvergne to the wharf, and the vegetable material was immediately carried to the first floor of the central building, where it was worked. The first operations of laying line (see pages 26-27 for details) produced ropes that were subsequently steamed and tarred. These two last operations were crucial: the humidity of the steaming room softened the rope in order to make it run smoothly through the pulleys, and the hot tarring made it rotproof. Once dry, this tar continued to stain everything it touched, and drove topmen to despair because, during their time of compulsory service in the Royal Navy, they could not manage to keep their hands clean for more than a few seconds. Ropes manufactured in this way measured the length of one cable, a unit of distance used in navigation which corresponds to 633 feet. The dimensions of workshops were determined to

This sophisticated piece of nautical equipment is called a "cluster of pulleys": it is designed for a low point in a square sail.

allow the manufacturing of ropes of this "standard" length. In fact, the Royal Rope Factory of Rochefort was not the only supplier for the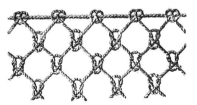

The main problem in manufacturing a net: to make knots identical in size.

Royal Navy, for the arsenal in Toulon had its own workshops as well. After the Revolution, the volume of rope provided began to decrease.

The Closing of the Factory

Then, in the nineteenth century, the development of steam navigation destroyed the strategic importance of the Rope Factory of Rochefort. The arsenal slowly declined to the advantage of those in Brest and Lorient, and in 1926 it closed. During the German occupation the port of Rochefort suffered serious damage, and the rope factory burned down in 1944. Fortunately, the navy, aware of the historic value of the premises, initiated restoration works in 1964. Today, the Factory shelters several administrative bodies such as the Conservatoire du littoral et des rivages lacustres [Seashore and Lakeshore Conservation League], the Ligue pour la protection des oiseaux [Bird Protection League] as well as the Centre international de la mer [International Center for the Sea]; the latter offers a fascinating permanent exhibition dedicated to the manufacture of ropes.

In theory nothing is simpler than the manufacture of a net: it is composed of diamond-shaped links, assembled by the extremely simple single-sheet bend. At a time when machines did not exist, tying hundreds of identical knots side by side, row after row, demanded extraordinary experience, infallible vision, as well as close attention. And even today this holds true for fishermen when they have to repair a torn trawl at sea.

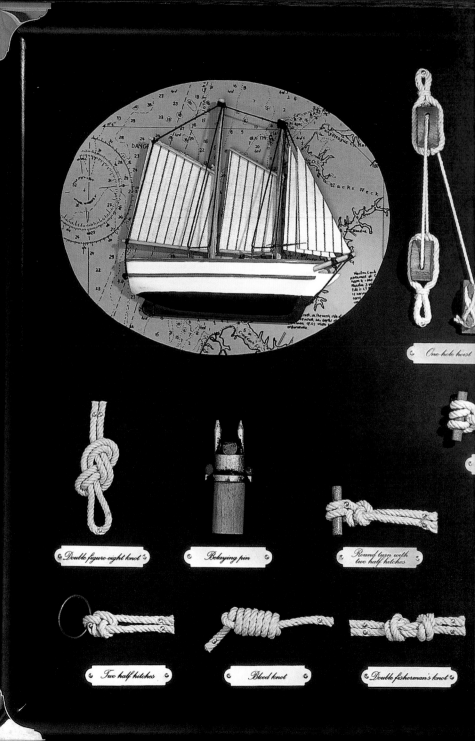

One-hole hoist

Double figure-eight knot

Belaying pin

Round turn with
two half hitches

Two half hitches

Blood knot

Double fisherman's knot

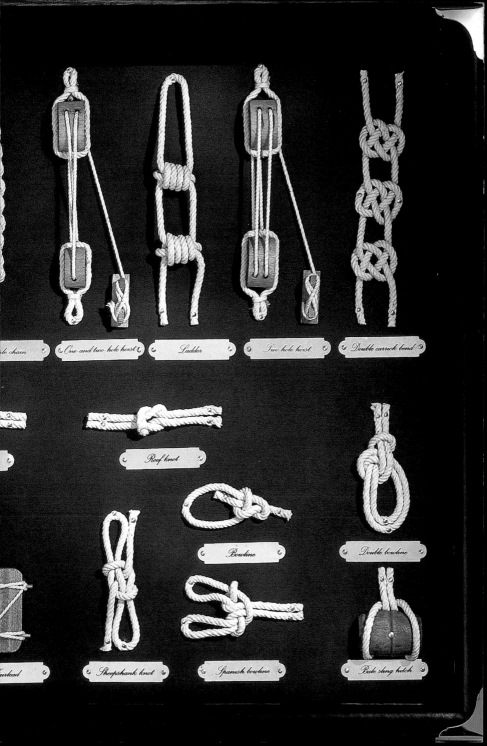

le chain   One and two-hole hoist   Ladder   Two-hole hoist   Double carrick bend

Reef knot

Double bowline

Bowline

rlead   Sheepshank knot   Spanish bowline   Bale sling hitch

Traditional Ropes

Whatever the material used, old ropes were all laid lines, that is, made of fibers that were twisted and then laid upon others. Ropes can be categorized by diameter as well as by the fiber chosen to make them and by the way they are laid. The special characteristics of the type of rope (hemp, Manila, coir, cotton, or sisal) helped to determine the option for each according to its intended use.

Hemp, Queen among Fibers for Ropes

Hemp has always been considered ideal. Because of its strength, flexibility, and average elasticity, this brown-colored rope makes a good shock absorber in case of sudden tension (for example, because wind is variable it was used for sails' sheets), but it does not stretch to the point where halyards must constantly be rehoisted. But not all ship owners could afford to buy hemp for their ships.

Manila hemp, recognizable by its rougher appearance, was less costly, but it proved a little less strong and flexible than hemp. However, since it was lighter and dried faster than hemp, it had the advantage of being longer lasting. Thus, it presented a good quality-to-cost ratio.

Sisal hemp, which also produces white string for packaging, has always been considered an admittedly cheap but fairly unreliable rope. However, two qualities of sisal can be identified: its lightness and its good resistance to bad weather.

Coir, made of coconut fibers, is even less strong. On the other hand, it is very light (it can float easily) and elastic. These two characteristics make this material ideal for mooring ropes and ground tackle.

LEFT:
A rope-maker's workshop in the first half of the twentieth century. The large wheel used for making rope was manually operated: just like the rigging of entire fleets!

TOP:
A branch of hemp. Its ligneous fibers were the ones to be spun.

A hawser made in this fashion allowed for very sophisticated maritime operations.

Cotton ropes have never been used for anything other than sails' sheets for the yachts of the past. Its main disadvantage is that it stretches too much. However, being flexible, it runs efficiently through sail pulleys. Above all, its soft touch is suitable for the hands of urban yachtsmen.

The Principle of Elasticity

Whatever the plant used, the raw material for rope comes in the form of a mass of tangled fibers, which need to be carded, combed, and then spun. After the first two operations are done, fibers are obtained which are ready to be spun. The longer fibers are the best and their quality is classified as "first string" (premier brin). In French, it is the origin of the expression gabier of premier brin, which used to designate experienced sailors in the times of sailing vessels. A second combing produces a new set of shorter fibers, which produces less strong and less uniform ropes; these are called the "second string." The residue is called tow; spun and twisted, it becomes the cord used for caulking hulls and decks.

The fibers are then put together and twisted to produce a continuous yarn. This operation is called laying. How does it work? By twisting the plant fibers in the same direction to form a yarn, we make an incalculable number

It is to Norwegian tar that we owe the peculiar odor of traditional-styled rigging, a balsamic scent that slightly resembles aloe and licorice. In reality, the tar comes more frequently from Finland and Sweden. However, the Norwegians specialized in the trade of this vegetable tar, which was obtained by burning the wood from conifers to cinders. After being soaked in hot tar, ropes and wood are made rotproof by the properties of this thick liquid.

of minute springs, which get tangled at the same time as they try to relax. Twisting several yarns together the direction opposite the first twisting to get a strand, then laying these strands atop each other and twisting in the direction opposite the last operation, the spring movement is thwarted, and thus a stabilized rope is produced.

From the Small Yarn to the Huge Hawser

The first thread, the basic element of all ropes, is called a yarn. It is itself made of two or three threads twisted from the left to the right. Traditionally, the yarn's diameter is a minimum of one millimeter ($\frac{1}{25}$ inch) to a maximum of nine millimeters (about $\frac{1}{3}$ inch).

A stopper knot keeps a rope's cut end from fraying. If you want to avoid the bump made by the knot, use a single wall knot or a back splice.

By twisting the yarns upon themselves, we obtain a strand. According to the strength and the diameter of the rope we want to obtain, we use more or fewer yarns. The strands are twisted in the opposite direction in relation to the yarns, that is, from the right to the left.

Rope is made by twisting three or four strands from left to right. A hawser is an especially thick rope for mooring and hauling. The hawsers designed to moor large ships have a diameter of about 3 to 12 inches.

Even thicker are cable-laid and cable: the former is between about 6 ½ to 13 ½ inches in diameter, and the latter is even thicker. Made of hawsers, they are twisted from right to left. A rope's strands can be used to make small temporary lashings, to make rigging trimmings in order to prevent sails from wearing out when in contact with stays, etc. But for these small tasks, new rope was never used: old rope from well-worn rigging was recycled. On board old sailing vessels, the rule was not to waste anything.

The Lost Art of Seafaring with Laid Line

I f left free, the end of a rope will untwist by itself. Tying a stopper knot—in most cases a well-tightened overhand knot is effective—is not always a satisfactory solution, because the bump this adds to the rope prevents it from running through pulleys and other bull's-eye blocks. There are two ways of fixing it: through whipping (common or West Country whipping) or through splicing.

To Protect the End of a Rope

Whipping is a tied wrapping made with thin cord usually coated with wax or pitch, which is often called "whipping twine." There are several ways of whipping. On thin ropes, the simplest and definitely most effective method, although not the most aesthetic, is West Country whipping. It consists of tying a series of overhand knots over several centimeters, starting from a few millimeters to one centimeter from the end of the rope. In general, the length of a whipping equals two or three times the diameter of the rope.

The most aesthetic is palm-and-needle whipping. It consists of winding the whipping thread tightly around the end of the rope. Then one passes a needle parallel to each one of the strands that make the rope, and each time the whipping is surrounded by two or three firmly tightened turns. Whatever the type of whipping chosen, it should barely increase the diameter of the rope.

But whipping, even West Country whipping, will eventually wear out. The only permanent way to keep a laid line from fraying is to splice it. There are a number of ways to make a splice, but the principle is always the same: a certain length of rope (four to six times its diameter) must be untwisted and each one of the undone strands must be interwoven with those that are still twisted. It can also be said that this is a form of weaving.

On ropes of small diameter and poor quality, it is easy to twist the rope in the opposite direction of its lay in order to make a space to slip the running strands under the standing ones. In general, however, it is advisable to use a tool called a marlinespike specially designed for separating the standing strands.

The Art of Splicing

Originally, the marlinespike was a thick, pointed tool that would be slipped between the strands to separate them. This tool was made of metal or hard wood. Today, marlinespikes are always hollow and made of metal. The marlinespike is put in between two strands, separating them. The running strand of the splice is slipped through the hollow of the marlinespike, placed under tension, and the tool is removed: the strand is in place and all that remains is to tighten it. How is a splice made? An explanation in writing would be woefully inadequate; it is necessary to see it done in order to

The short and long splices allow two ropes to be joined end to end.

understand the succession of hand movements that lead to such an aesthetic weaving. Briefly, here is the principle: to splice a rope upon itself, making a back splice, start by tying the strands together by turning them over and forming with each one an intertwined braid in the next (this is what is called a single wall knot). In this way, the rope is "stopped," and the back splice will further firmly secure the knot. To finish the back splice, slip each free strand into the twisted strand in front of it. Then tighten the splice very firmly. With a three-strand rope, three passes are generally sufficient.

The same technique can be used to make an eye at the end of the rope; this is called an eye splice. It is possible to attach a shackle to the eye in order to connect an anchor, a chain, a metal cable, and so on to the rope. Also, another rope can be tied on the eye by means of a sheet bend. Usually, the eye splice is made on a grommet, a protection designed to prevent the rope in the eye from wearing and tearing. To make an eye splice, untwist the end of the rope, lay it in the groove of the grommet, and then interweave the unlaid strands with the standing strands. Finally, the short splice allows two ropes to be joined end to end. Each one of them is unlaid a certain length, all strands are tucked into the other rope, and several passes such as those described above are made.

A topman's knife can be recognized by the square shape of its blade. Whether it has a fixed blade and is carried inside a sheath, or is collapsible like a pocketknife, the nautical knife always has a trapezoid-shaped blade. In the era of the great sailing ships, most captains would have the point of the blade of each topman's knife broken before setting sail to minimize the consequences of the inevitable brawls onboard. This is why naval blacksmiths started to forge blades without points from the outset.

Usually, an eye splice is reinforced by a metal grommet that protects it from friction.

Modern Ropes:
Synthetic and Plaited

The hemp, Manila, coir, and sisal ropes of long ago are followed by today's ropes of polyester, polyamide, aramid fiber, Vectran™, and others. Each material has its own specific use.

Polyester, the most commonly used of these materials, is as useful for halyards as it is for sheets and spinnaker braces. It withstands seawater and ultraviolet rays very well, offers good resistance to stretching, and generally is strong enough for most tasks.

Polypropylene, very light (which is what makes it practical) and very cheap, serves only as towing line and anchor lines for small boats. It is very slippery to touch and does not tolerate friction well.

Polyamide is quite elastic, which makes it the ideal material for mooring and lashing. However, it is sensitive to friction as well; one has to make sure to protect lines and lashing at all friction points.

Choosing the Best Material

High-quality polyethylene is marketed under the brand names Dyneema™ and Spectra™. Its resistance to stretching, its lightness, and its resistance to seawater and ultraviolet rays make it a good material for halyards. But this choice represents a significant investment.

Aramid fiber does not stretch at all, no matter the tension on it. It is the material used in halyards and running tackle on competition boats. On the other hand, it does not have good resistance to ultraviolet rays and being compressed by pulley sheaves (which must be larger than average): thus, it is necessary

LEFT:
On the deck of a modern sailing boat, powerful winches allow a young woman to control huge sails.

BELOW:
The sheet bend makes it possible to join ropes of different texture and diameter.

33

LEFT:
Bowline made
on a three-ply
mooring line.
The aesthetics of
nautical knots
never fails to
seduce.

to change ropes made with this fiber regularly.

Vectran offers the same advantages and is designed for the same uses: halyards and running tackle.

Ropes made of synthetic material are easier to "stop" than those made of vegetable fibers: melting the end to join the fibers together is enough. However, this operation demands a certain care, particularly when fusing the core and the sheath (see below).

To prevent a synthetic braided rope from fraying, here is the best way to proceed:

- measure off the length of rope needed and wrap adhesive tape tightly around the rope where the cut will be made;
- heat up a blade that is heat safe (for example, a kitchen knife or the blade of a metal saw);
- cut slowly with the blunt edge of the blade. In this way, the fibers melt uniformly and join together well;
- once the rope is cut and fused, it is a good idea to make a short incision in the fused part (about one to two centimeters ($2/5$ to $4/5$ inches)) in the form of a cross with a heated blade in order to join the core of the rope to its exterior braid. Usually, this is enough to keep the rope from fraying.

This method is simple, but it does not prevent the rope from fraying after a while. Ideally, the end should be whipped (as described above) after it is fused. The whipping should end several millimeters from the end of the rope; the end of the rope should then be melted again to form a small bump that will be folded over the last turns of the whipping. If we want to finish a plaited rope with an eye, the splice is not impossible, but only experts are able to do it. On the other hand, anybody can do sewing-whipping. The most common technique, which is very effective, consists of placing the two parts of the rope that wrap around the grommet side by side and then sewing them with thick whipping thread. If it is impossible to stitch through the core of the rope, one must stitch through the rope on each side at a third of its width.

Nylon ropes are laid in the same way hemp ones were in the past. However, the manufacturing of plaited ropes is very unusual: a core of parallel strands is covered with a sheath, and only the latter is plaited by means of eight, sixteen, or sometimes thirty-two strands. Also, certain high-resistance ropes are composed of a core covered with two sheaths: they are called "double plaited."

This stitching will keep the two parts in position so that all one must do is sew along a length about three or four times the diameter of the rope, tying each turn tightly.

A Matter of Maintenance

To keep a synthetic rope in good condition, first we need to avoid damaging it, and for that we need to limit friction points aboard: trimming the rigging and the turnbuckles prevents jib sheets from chafing at each tack. Moorings and anchor cables, however, must be passed through sections of hose where they are in contact with fairleads, the quay, etc., in order to protect them.

By reversing a rope regularly, we displace points of strain and make its two ends work alternately; it will last twice as long. Rinse ropes in fresh water whenever possible: while synthetic material does not decay under the effect of salt, salt "burns" synthetic material, and salt crystals wear out fibers little by little.

Overhand Knot or Thumb Knot

Not very nautical, but can be useful

USEFUL FACTS

A half hitch is an overhand knot that has one of its ends "turned over": it's the first step in making something fast. It's often the case that an overhand knot appears on its own on a rope that has been left in a tangle. It must be undone before it's used, otherwise it risks getting stuck somewhere, causing a bad move! To undo a very tight overhand knot, the only solution is to stick a fid or spike into it.

Brief History

This is the knot that everyone knows how to make, but which people are frequently unable to undo. In fact, if it is tied tightly, becomes wet with salt water, and then dries, it forms an almost permanent knot. However, you must not use it as a stop knot: if it is not tied tightly enough, it undoes itself. Tied too tightly, it lacks volume and risks getting stuck inside a pulley instead of stopping on the outside, against the inlet fitting. On the other hand, as you can see on pages 60 and 61, the overhand knot reveals all its usefulness when it becomes a half hitch.

Simple Overhand Loop

To make a stopper knot in the middle of a rope

1

USEFUL FACTS
This overhand knot,
made with a doubled
rope, comes very
naturally to the fingers.
The ring it forms also
serves well as a good-
quality handle. It is
important to make sure
the short end of the rope
extends beyond the knot,
otherwise the knot may
come undone.

2

Brief History

It is easy to make, but impossible to untie if it tightens up; its turns
resemble the shape of a clenched fist. This knot will not budge, especially if the rope is very taut. This results in limited usage, but one to
which it is perfectly suited: you can use it on a length of rope which
you absolutely need to isolate the damaged part. Don't forget, though,
upon arriving at port, to replace the defective rope. Continuing to use a
damaged rope with a large stopper knot would present a significant risk.

38

Figure-Eight Knot
Of good bulk, it holds well and is easily undone

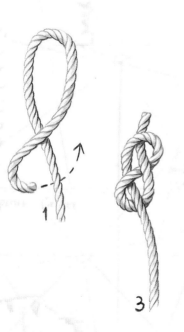

USEFUL FACTS

This easily made knot should be considered the stopper knot par excellence. If by chance it is very tight and saturated with salt water, the easiest way to undo it is to twist it into itself. Leave at least 7 ¾ inch between the knot and the end of the rope in order to have enough to grasp when the "eight" is stuck in a pulley or fairlead.

Brief History

No rope used in a pulley, hoist, or fairlead system should be able to free itself. If it does, the maneuver is spoiled and cannot be redone: a sail flapping in the wind that you cannot control or a halyard come out of its pulley which is fixed at the top of the mast. To avoid disasters like this, the stopper knot must be tight enough so it doesn't unravel itself but also big enough so it doesn't get jammed in its lead. The figure-eight knot is the one made at the end of sheets (the rope that trims the sail) that are frequently taken down. In fact, it is easy to undo, even when saturated with dried salt water.

Heaving-Line Knot
For a permanent and bulky stop knot

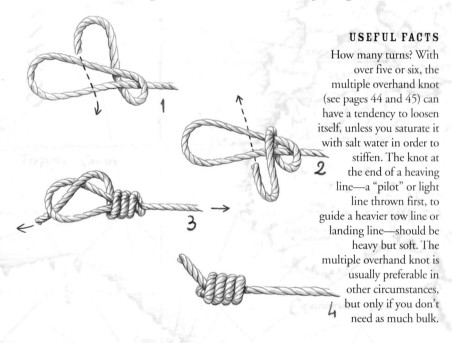

USEFUL FACTS

How many turns? With over five or six, the multiple overhand knot (see pages 44 and 45) can have a tendency to loosen itself, unless you saturate it with salt water in order to stiffen. The knot at the end of a heaving line—a "pilot" or light line thrown first, to guide a heavier tow line or landing line—should be heavy but soft. The multiple overhand knot is usually preferable in other circumstances, but only if you don't need as much bulk.

Brief History

Its elegant form is reminiscent of the multiple overhand knot on pages 44 and 45. But the heaving-line knot is bulkier and does not run the risk of getting stuck in a pulley when it is used to stop the end of the rope permanently; it can be employed on fixed hoists (large-sail or downhaul) which are found aboard sailing vessels. In practice, it is wise to give it a good number of turns for added bulk so that it is easier to grasp the knot.

Multiple Overhand Knot (Blood Knot)

For a permanent and reliable knot

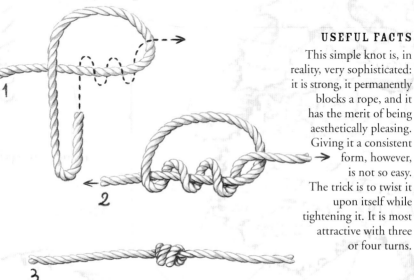

USEFUL FACTS

This simple knot is, in reality, very sophisticated: it is strong, it permanently blocks a rope, and it has the merit of being aesthetically pleasing. Giving it a consistent form, however, is not so easy. The trick is to twist it upon itself while tightening it. It is most attractive with three or four turns.

Brief History

This knot was tied at the ends of Capuchin monks' belts, and surgeons may have used this knot to tie off severed blood vessels. The trick is to pull on both ends of the rope at the same time while twisting them in opposite directions, so that the knot works itself slowly tighter without tangling. It can be used as a stopper knot as well as decoration at the end of a cord.

Granny Knot
A knot for educational purposes only

1

2

3

USEFUL FACTS
Mountain climbers also know a granny knot, but it has nothing to do with sailors' granny knots: it is a very useful overhand knot made in a belaying rope which serves to fasten a hook to an eye or a strap ring. Granny knot or reef knot? To find out, give it a try!

Brief History

The granny knot is also known as a cow's knot, and as its earthy name indicates, it has no more purpose aboard a sailing ship than a bovine. So it really serves no purpose, then? Of course not! But its only virtues are of the educational sort. To put it plainly, it serves to demonstrate to novices what a failed reef knot looks like, and this is a useful exercise: the granny knot looks similar to the reef knot. But if you place the granny knot under stress, it loosens immediately. Now you understand what you must *not* do. Turn to pages 48 and 49.

Reef Knot

To combine two ropes of the same diameter

USEFUL FACTS

Its principal usage onboard: to join reef point to reef or to make something fast to a flat deck. If the reef knot is made with ropes of different diameters or textures, it may loosen. When tying a reef knot, ensure that each of the ropes enters and exits from the same side of the bight formed by the other rope.

Brief History

Be careful with this knot since it can loosen on its own if tension is put on it in the right direction. This may be accidental, but then this knot can turn out to be impossible to undo if you don't know how to "flip" it. Indeed, the person who can undo this reef knot is not necessarily an expert: the technique for "flipping" this knot consists of pulling on one of the lengths of rope that is perpendicular to the rope that is taut, as if you want to tear it away from the knot.

Simple Fisherman's Knot
Universal, but often difficult to undo

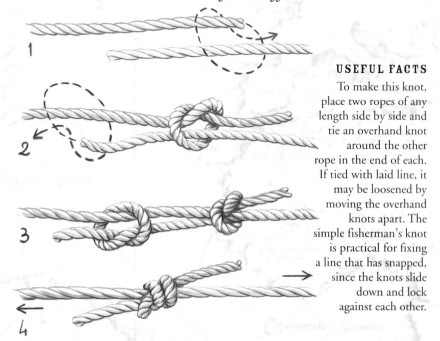

1

2

3

4

USEFUL FACTS

To make this knot, place two ropes of any length side by side and tie an overhand knot around the other rope in the end of each. If tied with laid line, it may be loosened by moving the overhand knots apart. The simple fisherman's knot is practical for fixing a line that has snapped, since the knots slide down and lock against each other.

Brief History

Originally created to join fishing lines together, this knot allows you to join ropes of different rigidity, texture, and (to a certain extent) diameter end to end. With stiff rope, it undoes itself easily: it is enough to pull apart the two simple knots which make it up, in this case overhand knots. Avoid making it on ropes of very different diameters, for example, with a fine line and a thick cable: the "small" knot risks passing through the "big."

Double Fisherman's Knot
To join two ropes of the same diameter

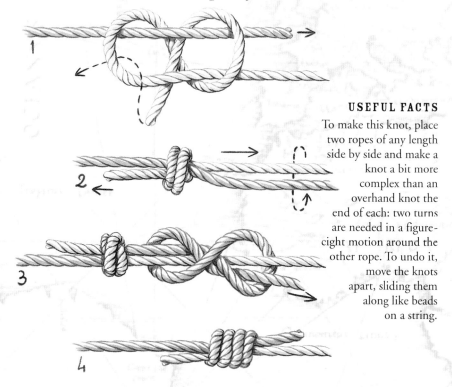

USEFUL FACTS

To make this knot, place two ropes of any length side by side and make a knot a bit more complex than an overhand knot the end of each: two turns are needed in a figure-eight motion around the other rope. To undo it, move the knots apart, sliding them along like beads on a string.

Brief History

It is not only sailors and fishermen who swear by this knot: mountain climbers have also come to use it for joining two ropes end to end. However, it would be a mistake to imagine that this knot is more solid because it is doubled. The two turns create a shock-absorbing effect when the rope is subjected to tension: the first turn is crushed upon itself and the second ensures the grip. As a result, it is always easy to undo the knot.

Double-Sheet Bend
To join two ropes of different diameters end to end

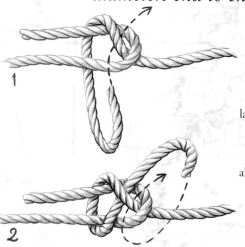

Brief History

A variation of the double-sheet bend is known as a weaver's knot because it serves to join two threads. It is also called the net knot because it is used to make nets. Topmen of long ago adopted it to fasten the sheet to a loop of rope arranged at an angle to the sail. Today, the clews on modern sails are no longer made this way. But this knot remains very useful for joining a pennant to its halyard. While the weaver's knot and the net knot are always made with one turn, the double-sheet bend used to join two cables is always made with two turns.

Two Bowlines
Easy to undo, for all ropes

USEFUL FACTS

This is actually two simple bowlines tied together (see pages 76 and 77). If you cannot master the bowline, forget about the two bowlines for the time being. Do not hesitate to make large loops in each of the bowlines: you obtain good shock absorption of jolts from doing this.

Brief History

Is this the most universal knot used to join two ropes? Yes, but it proves to be quite heavy, which is important when using it in ground tackle. In bad weather, in order to guarantee a good hold on the anchor, one often uses two ropes end to end. However, there is always the possibility that a knot will slip under the violent jolts caused by waves and wind; this can happen with a sheet bend and more so with a reef knot. As for the double fisherman's knot made with stiff rope, it can prove difficult to undo after severe stress has been placed on it. And so we have the two bowlines.

Carrick Bend
Attractive, but infrequently used

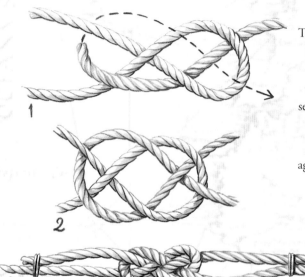

USEFUL FACTS
The carrick bend will not stay on its own: it needs to be finished with lashing made of thin cord. The carrick bend serves as a shock absorber between two ropes or cables, the interlaced parts working easily against each other despite the stiffness of the cable. The lashing of thin cord can simply be a succession of clove hitches (see pages 64 and 65).

Brief History
For connoisseurs of wooden sailing ships, the carrick bend was used to moor old vessels with their enormous cables. For lovers of military uniforms, it is a vestige of trimmings decorating buttonholes, and historians recognize it as a symbol of fidelity adopted by the Savoy family. In any case, they all agree in considering this the most aesthetic of all knots. Its use at sea, however, is very limited: it is good only for quickly joining two parts of a broken metal cable.

Round Turn and Two Half Hitches
Simple, quick, and very useful

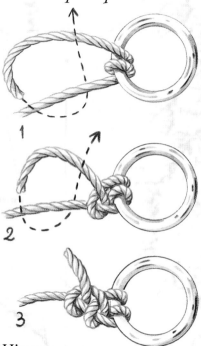

1

2

3

USEFUL FACTS
Note that the French term for the round turn is "tour mort," or "dead turn." Perhaps this means that after the first turn (the living), you make a second (the dead) intended to stop it. It is this second turn which you must make quickly, before tension is put on the rope. If the knot is untied afterwards, the half hitches can be replaced by a bowline.

Brief History
The sailing ship arrives at the dock, but the wind tries to push it away; the canoe arrives at the riverbank, but the strong current only wants to sweep it away. You must quickly make your vessel fast, even if it means redoing it afterwards in a more sophisticated way. The round turn with two half hitches is the quickest and surest maneuver. Even if the boat pulls on its line, you can still tie it. You must take the time to tighten the two half hitches that lock it, because this type of knot will not resist jolts for very long.

Two Doubled Half Hitches
To moor in the case of extreme urgency

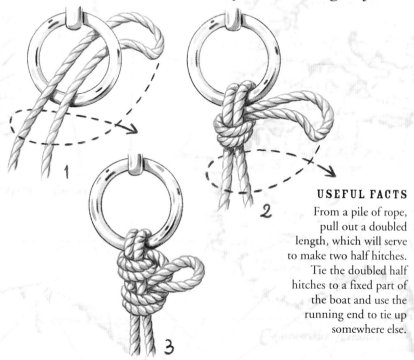

USEFUL FACTS

From a pile of rope, pull out a doubled length, which will serve to make two half hitches. Tie the doubled half hitches to a fixed part of the boat and use the running end to tie up somewhere else.

Brief History

Catastrophe! You arrive at the dock and your landing lines are tangled. This can happen even to the best of crews, when, for example, they embark on a boat used previously by less conscientious sailors. From this "bowl of spaghetti" on the deck, pull out a sufficient length for landing the boat, even if the ends of the rope are still tangled in a pile. Make the two doubled half hitches on a sturdy part of the boat and throw the pile onto the dock to make it fast to a cleat. Then put yourself to work at straightening out this unacceptable muddle.

Clove Hitch

Self-tightening knot to make anywhere

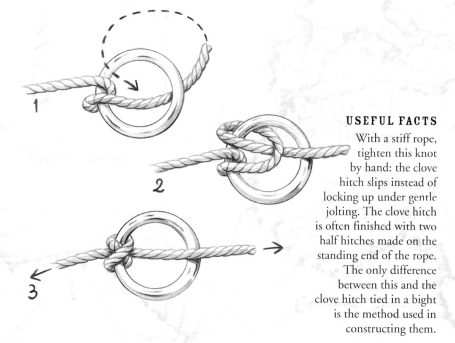

USEFUL FACTS

With a stiff rope, tighten this knot by hand: the clove hitch slips instead of locking up under gentle jolting. The clove hitch is often finished with two half hitches made on the standing end of the rope. The only difference between this and the clove hitch tied in a bight is the method used in constructing them.

Brief History

There is a mystery surrounding this knot. Even though some sailors call this a capstan knot, they know full well that it was never used to fasten the anchor cable to the capstan, a winch intended to pull up the mooring. The clove hitch (which is its more common name) is a self-tightening knot, which means that the more you pull on the cable, the more it locks up. The difficulty for the novice is to memorize the specific order in which the rope must be passed and crossed.

Double Clove Hitch
A clove hitch that resists jolts

USEFUL FACTS

With a stiff rope, tighten this knot by hand: in this way, you'll be certain that the double clove hitch will not slip when it is supposed to lock up. Nothing prevents you from finishing the double clove hitch with two half hitches made on the standing end of the rope. Do not confuse the double clove hitch with a succession of three clove hitches.

Brief History

If the mooring must withstand jolts, one could worry that the clove hitch tied in a bight might not tighten too much (at each pull, in the case of supple rope). In this case, they constrict and make the knot difficult to undo later. On the other hand, if the rope is made of a stiff synthetic material, it has a tendency to loosen itself at each jolt and may end up slipping. The answer consists of inserting a round turn between each of the two half hitches that make up the clove hitch.

Using a double clove hitch in cases where the rope will be subjected to jolts may result in overtightening of the knot, especially if supple rope is used. However, if using stiff rope, the double clove hitch is preferable to the clove hitch because the round turn inserted between the half hitches serves to help lock the rope in place.

Clove Hitch Tied in a Bight
A clove hitch to make on a mooring post

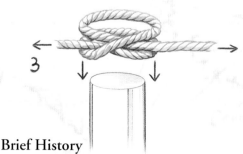

USEFUL FACTS

A hand movement to memorize: you must, if you do not go to sea every day, practice this one often. The clove hitch tied in a bight is often finished with two additional half hitches made on the standing end of the rope. The only difference between this and the clove hitch (see pages 64 and 65) is the method used in constructing them.

Brief History

Long ago, landing lines were caught on mooring posts. A single knot was allowed in this action, and the move, not much in use today, was somewhat magical. Clove hitches tied in a bight are made up of two reversed loops laid atop each other, which has a self-blocking effect. The technique: make a first loop which you allow to fall over the mooring post. Then make a second, in the direction opposite to the first, and place it atop the first on the post.

Fisherman's Bend
(Grapnel Knot, Anchor Bend)
To fasten a small anchor to ground tackle

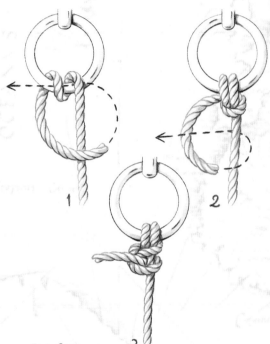

USEFUL FACTS
You may make three or four turns to distribute the tension over a larger surface and thus limit the effect of abrasion even more. The important thing is to tighten the knot well by hand so that any jolts are immediately absorbed by the elasticity of the rope and not by the turns. Some people replace the securing half hitches with a bowline. Why not?

Brief History
The worst enemy of working lines is what sailors call "chafing," namely, wear and tear from friction and rubbing. The fisherman's bend resists this rubbing because it tightly hugs the metal with its two round turns. Because of the round turns, the knot is not in direct contact with the ring. The working end of the rope passes between the two round turns and the ring: the knot's holding power is therefore obtained through its self-locking effect, and the two half hitches made on the standing end of the rope are for extra security only.

Lark's Head Hitch
When both ends of the rope have tension on them

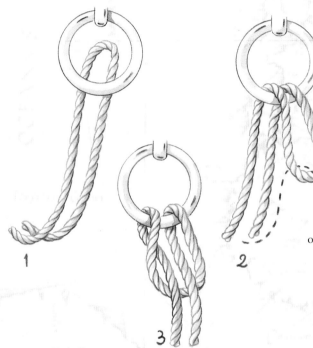

1

2

3

USEFUL FACTS

When you join a net to its bolt rope, you may choose to use a clove hitch or a lark's head hitch. The lark's head hitch is also an easy way to hang ropes of short length. It is even practical for joining a rope to a whistle or a bearing compass to your hand.

Brief History

You are completely correct to ask what this feathered creature is doing in this story. Hoping to catch their sailing instructors off balance, many trainees ask this very question, only to find themselves being asked in return to make this knot. Very proud of themselves, they succeed the first time. And the instructor then explains with great pleasure that this knot is so easy to make that anyone with a birdbrain, like a lark, can manage to do it quite well. The lark's head hitch is used when both ends of the rope must be under strain, as in the case of double mooring.

Timber Hitch

The knot of lumberjacks becomes nautical

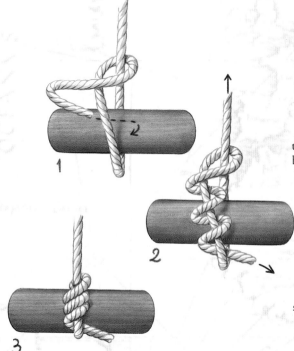

USEFUL FACTS

Make the first tightening by hand to ensure that the tension is distributed over the entire length of the knot. For this knot to be useful, the diameter of the rope must be much less than that of the "wood." If it isn't, use the clove hitch instead.

If the rope will be subjected to jerking, the timber hitch can be preceded with a simple half hitch, which will serve as a shock absorber.

Brief History

Originally, this knot was used to haul a log between the place where the tree was felled and the road where it would be loaded onto a trailer. It allowed the log to be aligned with the trailer. However, this can be a problem aboard ship if you don't want the object to be able to twist freely. The main advantage of this knot is that it is self-tightening and very secure since the knot is distributed over a good length of "wood."

Bowline (1)
Undoes easily, even after high tension

USEFUL FACTS
You think you really know how to make a bowline? Try it with your eyes closed, then with your hands behind your back! To remember how to make it: the working end that forms the knot passes alternately over and under the standing rope. On stiff rope that will be submitted to changing tension, allow the working end to extend well past the knot itself, or else the bowline may come undone.

Brief History
In French, the bowline is called the "noeud de chaise," or "chair knot," because the loop formed by this knot was used at one time to suspend a topman who would have to carry out a repair in the rigging, without any point of support. But in reality, the bowline has always been the best way to make a loop that does not slip. This might be very difficult for a landlubber to believe, and it leaves a person to imagine that its discovery took some time. No doubt that when it was first created, it was welcomed as a grand invention.

Bowline (2)

A knot that makes itself on its own

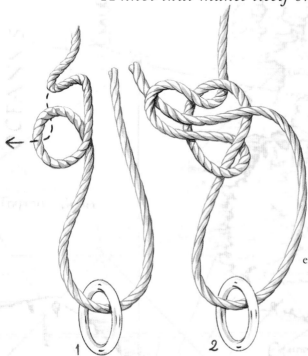

Brief History

A bowline is difficult to make when the line is under high tension, for example when trying to tie it on the towline of a vessel being pushed by wind or current. But it is possible to use precisely that tension to make the knot, as if by magic. The principle is to make a braided half hitch (see pages 108 and 109). Pass the working end of the rope through a mooring ring and then pass it through the loop formed by the braided half hitch. Once the rope is drawn tight, the braid closes up on the rope that passes through it and becomes a bowline.

Bowline on a Bight

The veritable bosun's chair

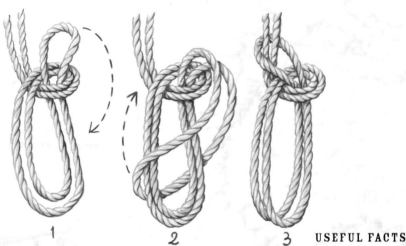

1 2 3

USEFUL FACTS

Though it may seem reliable when it is made in the classic way, a doubled bowline risks undoing itself if made that way. Therefore, make a bowline on a bight instead. For rigging, make a smaller loop than shown in the drawing, which is enlarged for detail. In practice, the bowline on a bight has only very limited use.

Brief History

This knot is truly intended for sitting, because the simple bowline knot is uncomfortable. With two loops, one is a bit more comfortable. Once settled, this knot will not come undone. Begin as if you are making a normal bowline, but with the rope doubled. In the second step, however, instead of making the turn around the standing end of the rope and coming back through the loop with the working end doubled, just slip the loop through the working bight.

Double Bowline
The most certain for hoisting in rigging

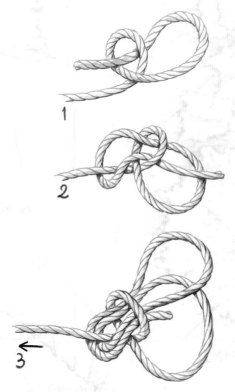

USEFUL FACTS

It is prudent to allow the working end of the rope in this knot to extend quite a bit beyond the knot; you can even make two or three half hitches with it to prevent the bowline from undoing itself accidentally. The crew member may sit on a life vest or cockpit cushion laid on the bottom loop so that the ascent on the rigging does not turn into a form of torture.

Brief History

The large loop is the seat, and the small loop is the back. The greatest risk of sitting in a bowline is slipping through the loop or falling backwards. To make this double bowline, the crewmember who is going to be hoisted in the rigging (for example) begins by making a simple bowline. He places this first loop around under his buttocks and, with the working end of the rope, makes another loop, adjusted around his waist.

Overhand Figure-Eight Loop (1)

A loop that is very easy to undo

USEFUL FACTS

For those who have never been able to master the bowline, the overhand figure-eight loop is an acceptable replacement. The shock absorption of this knot can prove useful, as when a mooring will be submitted to violent jolts during bad weather, for example. This knot is not so easy to make on big, stiff ropes.

Brief History

We come back to the simple overhand loop, whose usage we rejected because it was too difficult to undo after being under high tension. But by replacing the simple overhand knot with a figure-eight knot, we obtain a shock-absorbing effect. Therefore, this loop can be put under great strain while remaining much easier to undo than a bowline after-wards. The overhand figure-eight loop proves to be bulkier and requires a longer section of rope than the bowline, and that can be an important factor.

Overhand Figure-Eight Loop (2)

If you must make the loop on a ring

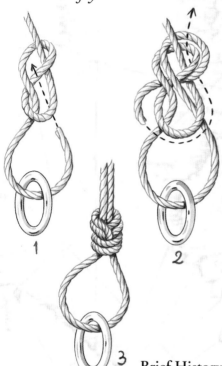

1

2

3

USEFUL FACTS

Make the first figure eight just loose enough so that after putting the working end through a ring, you can easily pass the working end back through the figure eight, paralleling its turns. This easy-to-memorize knot cannot be poorly made; this is an advantage because it is truly useful only in circumstances where one could yield to panic.

Brief History

The shock-absorbing quality of the overhand figure-eight loop is such that mountain climbers use it to join their belaying cord to their harness. To make your vessel fast to a ring on the quay and have some shock absorption in the rope, make a normal figure-eight knot at a point a bit more than twice the diameter of the desired loop from the end of the line. Pass the line through the ring, then pass the working end of the rope through the interlacings of the figure eight, paralleling its turns.

Towing Loop
A loop made in the middle of a rope

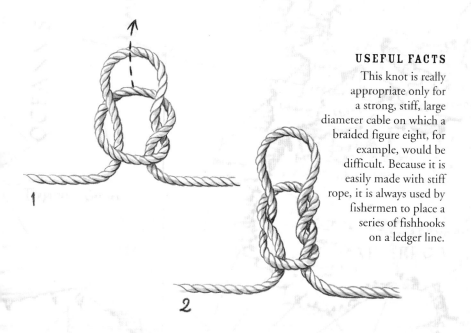

USEFUL FACTS

This knot is really appropriate only for a strong, stiff, large diameter cable on which a braided figure eight, for example, would be difficult. Because it is easily made with stiff rope, it is always used by fishermen to place a series of fishhooks on a ledger line.

Brief History

In the era of luggers, tramp sailing ships that went up the deepest estuaries, arrival at port was often made by towing the boat along a towpath. The crew spread themselves out on the towpath and, passing their shoulders through the loop made in this knot, pulled the boat to the quay. Of course, the importance of this knot is that it is made quickly and can be undone just as quickly; because of this, one can almost instantly move the pulling points on the tow.

Simple Running Knot
Very little rope needed for a reliable result

1

2

3

USEFUL FACTS
Note that if this knot is tied very tightly in a fine string, it can eventually cut that which it was intended to attach. To undo it when the loop is no longer needed, simply pull on the two ends of the rope. The simple overhand knot on the running end serving as a stopper is useful only on a fine and smooth string.

Brief History

When you do not know how to make knots but when you need a loop, this is the first method that comes to mind. However, it presents disadvantages when it constricts and clearly does not want to loosen, or when it slips and risks becoming undone. To keep it from loosening itself, use an overhand knot as a stopper. This is a makeshift hold, though, and you must learn to tie another knot (bowline, overhand figure-eight loop). But if you need to make a mooring or make something fast and have only a very short rope, consider the simple running knot: it will prove to be particularly economical.

Hangman's Noose
A sliding loop whose turns act as a stop

USEFUL FACTS

To pick up a mooring buoy in strong wind or current, prepare a large hangman's noose and drop it over the buoy as you approach it. This knot works best in stiff rope that does not have a tendency to constrict too much. In practice, four or five turns usually prove sufficient.

Brief History

The appearance of the hangman's noose is attributed to a torturer in the seventeenth century who, working in London, would "hang high and short until death ensued" many mutineers and pirates. He reckoned that seven turns were necessary for the proper functioning of this knot. But enough about its more sinister purposes—this sliding loop can be used today to lasso a faraway object. In fact, the more turns you give it, the more weighted the end of the rope will be, and the better its chance of reaching its target.

Running Bowline
A sliding loop that glides quickly without stopping

USEFUL FACTS

The fixed loop through which the rope runs must be just large enough so that only the rope and nothing else slides through it. If it is too large, the rope can get tangled up in it. Because the bowline knot that forms the fixed loop is not subject to any tension, it must be tightened by hand to ensure that it will not undo itself.

Brief History

This is a perfect sliding loop. The running bowline is ideal in cases where one needs a sliding loop that glides very well; for example, to deaden or make fast a sail that is flapping in the wind. As we can see at first glance, the running bowline is composed of a bowline through whose fixed loop the rope slides. Therefore, this knot can be undone easily.

Tarbuck Knot
For rope made of natural fiber

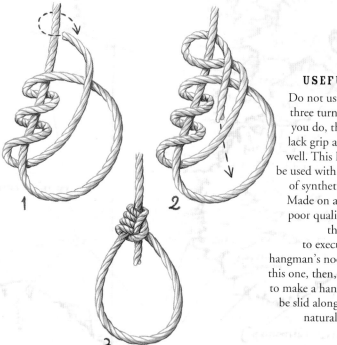

USEFUL FACTS

Do not use more than three turns, because if you do, this knot will lack grip and not slide well. This knot cannot be used with ropes made of synthetic materials. Made on a sisal line of poor quality, however, this is simpler to execute than the hangman's noose. Choose this one, then, if you need to make a handle that can be slid along a length of natural-fiber rope.

Brief History

With the revival of old riggings, one often finds ropes made of natural fiber. You might one day find yourself embarking on a Yemeni dhow, a Malaysian pran, a raft on the Lake Titicaca, or another small craft that has only fragile plant fiber rope. So, remember the tarbuck knot. Its particular configuration makes it constrict under high stress and tension and holds firmly. Thus, weak rope made of sisal, hemp, or cotton holds well instead of snapping.

Simple Chain
This knitting stitch is also of service on boats

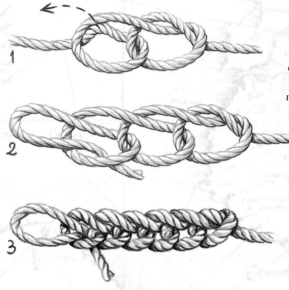

USEFUL FACTS

To tidy up a short length of rope, one can first fold it two or three times before making the chain: this is the technique used by mountaineers. To stop the chain and keep it from unraveling, pass the end of the rope through the last loop. When it comes time to undo it, one is often hard put to determine which end to free so that the chain undoes itself all on its own; every trick has its weakness.

Brief History

By using the simple chain, the length of a rope is shortened by one third. Sailors, who borrowed the chain from our knitting grandmothers and from the mountaineers who coiled their ropes in this way, used it to tidy up long ropes into a smaller volume. It is immediately useable: you need only pull on the chain to undo it. In practice, it is a succession of braided knots worked through each other repetitively.

Sheepshank (1)
In case dismasting occurs

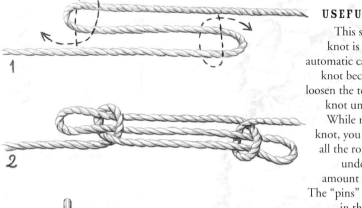

USEFUL FACTS

This sheepshank knot is called "the automatic casting-off" knot because if you loosen the tension, the knot undoes itself. While making the knot, you must keep all the rope or cable under a certain amount of tension. The "pins" positioned in the loops are intended to maintain the knot even if the tension is released, but they can be used only when the rope or cable is very rigid.

Brief History

Rarely used, because it requires that the shortened rope must always be kept taut, nonetheless it figures in all seafaring manuals. It is important to know because this knot with a curious name can save a ship. In fact, it is ideal if after a dismasting you want to construct a foresail rigging but can't easily use the original shrouds because they are too long for the sections of mast that you can still raise. This sheepshank knot is a useful solution in the event you don't own a pair of shroud shears and don't have the means to make grommets to fasten the new lengths.

Sheepshank (2)

A strange, but often necessary procedure

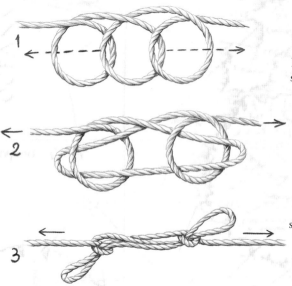

Brief History

This technique, in which three loops are passed through each other and transform as if by magic into a sheepshank knot, looks very suspicious. It seems to come right out of one of those old scouting books full of seductive "tricks" for which you try in vain to find a real use. Moreover, how does this knot resemble the shank of a sheep? It doesn't matter. This method is the only practical one when you need to shorten a very stiff cable, such as one made of a single strand of stainless steel.

Sheepshank (3)

*Even if the tension is removed,
it does not undo itself*

USEFUL FACTS

This method needs a little preparation: first, fold the part of the rope that will be used in the sheepshank in three. Then make a simple running knot (see pages 90 and 91) in the rope where you want the first bight to be. Dip the third bight into the running knot and pull the running knot tight to keep the bight from slipping out. With the running end, tie a running knot with the second bight fed through its loops and pull that running knot tight as well.

Brief History

It is out of the question to use this knot on a steel cable: rather, it requires a much more flexible rope so that you can tighten the running knots. Once the bights are passed through the running knots, they are "braided": it is between the two braids that the folds used to shorten the rope are stopped. In fact, this permanent sheepshank has the most limited use among the knots that are used to shorten a length of rope. It is used only when it is impossible to coil and hang the surplus line or wire which you cannot cut.

Mooring on a Cleat
The only good way of proceeding

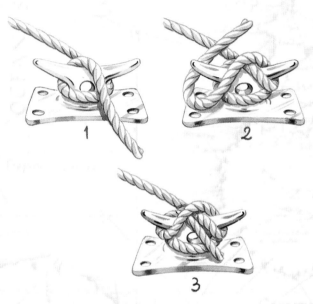

USEFUL FACTS

If the rope that is made fast on a cleat is likely to be cast off frequently or quickly (for example, a sheet or a mooring to which adjustments must be made very often), make a round turn around the cleat and then cross it with two figure eights on top of each other. If the rope does not need to be adjusted for a while (halyard, ground tackle), simply make a single figure eight and put a half hitch on top of it.

Brief History

On a boat, halyards, sheets, and moorings are fastened to cleats. On land, cleats serve to stop the halyard of a flag on its mast or the pull cord of a blinds. It is enough to put a turn around the cleat and then a figure eight, or so you might think. In reality, it may not be as simple as that. First, if it's a landing line, the person who unties it—perhaps in an emergency or in darkness—must be able to undo it as quickly as possible. In principle, the wraps on a cleat must therefore be made according to a standard method. Just like, on a sailboat, a specific halyard and a specific sheet are always placed on their own designated cleats.

Braided Half Hitch
You can undo it with one hand

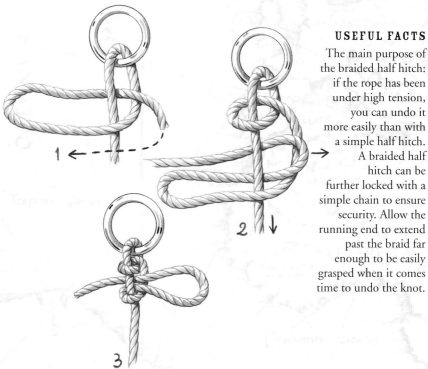

USEFUL FACTS
The main purpose of the braided half hitch: if the rope has been under high tension, you can undo it more easily than with a simple half hitch. A braided half hitch can be further locked with a simple chain to ensure security. Allow the running end to extend past the braid far enough to be easily grasped when it comes time to undo the knot.

Brief History

"One hand for you, one hand for the ship," goes the old saying that dates back to the era of the great sailing vessels, when the topmen balanced themselves on the yards, several dozen meters above the water, rolling and pitching because of a storm. In such cases one could fully appreciate the advantage of a knot that could be undone with one hand. In fact, the braided half hitch is none other than the simple knot you make each time you tie your shoelaces.

Bird's-Beak Knot
Knot that replaces a hoist pulley

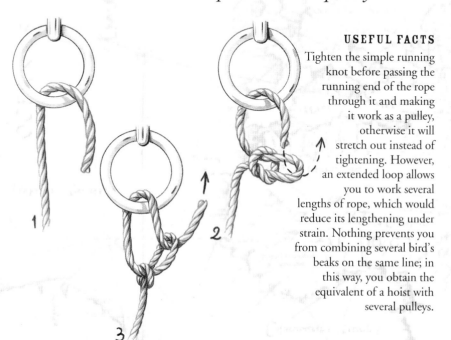

USEFUL FACTS
Tighten the simple running knot before passing the running end of the rope through it and making it work as a pulley, otherwise it will stretch out instead of tightening. However, an extended loop allows you to work several lengths of rope, which would reduce its lengthening under strain. Nothing prevents you from combining several bird's beaks on the same line; in this way, you obtain the equivalent of a hoist with several pulleys.

Brief History

If you want to lash something to the deck when you know the sea will be choppy, or when you must tighten a hoisting (for example, the tack of a foresail), the bird's beak allows you to improvise a hoist quickly. The loop which serves as a pulley is simply the beginning of a simple chain (see pages 98 and 99), or the simple running knot (page 90). This loop undoes itself easily when you feed the running end back through the loop and then pull on both ends of the rope. But if you must often redo the knot with the same end, you can replace the simple running knot with a more permanent bowline.

Square Turk's Head
Much easier to make than it appears

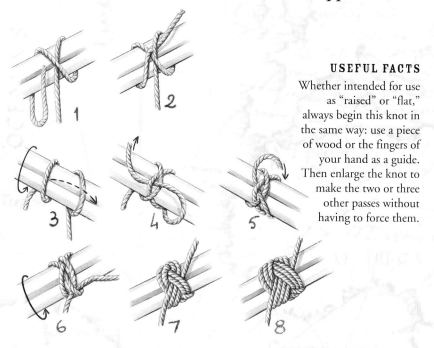

Brief History

The square Turk's head often appears among ornamental knots. However, it is not intended just for "beautification": it has many very precise uses. If you find it on a spoke of the ship's helm or at a precise point in its circle, it marks the "king spoke," or the position where the helm is straight. Made flat, it can serve as a mat to prevent the gravel of the quays from scoring wooden decks and the varnish in the cabin. It is also made around the fixed point of a flat deck pulley in order to absorb the shocks when it strikes the deck during maneuvers.

Monkey's Fist
More difficult to make than you think

USEFUL FACTS
Follow the steps illustrated on this page closely; do not mistake the directions shown in step two, when it is time to wrap across the first loops. There is the same risk of being misled at step three. Make the monkey's fist without tightening any of the wraps and then progressively pull it together as a whole.

Brief History

The monkey's fist heaving line is a light line, easily thrown from one boat to another or from a boat to the quay. It serves to pass a larger line that would have been impossible to throw directly. One of the ends of the heaving line is ballasted in order to be thrown far despite the wind. The monkey's fist, whose interlacings contain a lead ball (or a round pebble), weights one end of the line. A true monkey's fist heaving line is made on a line 6–10 millimeters in diameter. Made with a finer line, this knot allows you to make a key ring or a tab to pull a zipper.

GLOSSARY

A

ANCHOR POST: wooden post to which a rope may be lashed.

B

BEARING COMPASS: compass intended to measure the orientation of seamarks in relation to the north to establish a point of reference.

BECKET: a ring made in the strop of a pulley situated at the bottom of the pulley to lash the standing end of a rope to a hoist.

BEND, TO: to bind or make fast a rope to another object (such as another rope) by using a hitch or a bend.

BOAT HOOK: a hook mounted at the end of a pole, used to pull or push boats toward or away from a landing, to pick up a mooring, etc.

BULL'S-EYE TRUCK: piece of wood in which a hole is made and used as a pulley.

BUOY: a float.

C

CAPSTAN: vertical winch used primarily to raise the anchor.

CAULKING: operation consisting of forcing tow into the seams between pieces or planks of wood in order to ensure watertightness.

CHAFING: the rubbing of two objects against each other, bringing about premature wear.

CLEAT: a piece of wood or metal intended to fasten a sheet, a mooring, a halyard.

CLIPPER: a very fast sailing vessel used at the end of the nineteenth century.

COASTER/COASTING VESSEL: a ship that navigates along the coastline.

COME ABOUT, TO: a maneuver consisting of changing the direction of a sailboat so that it receives the wind from the other side.

D

DEADMAN: pole buried under water, connected to a chain, which is then connected to a buoy

DIPPING LUG: trapezoid sail whose tack is situated at the foot of the mast, set in the middle of a yard, a third of which is found in front of the mast.

F

FAIRLEAD: a fitting that guides mooring cables or rigging.

FORESAIL: a foresail rigging is an improvised rigging.

G

GAFF TOPSAIL: a sail set above the fore and aft sail (in other words, a trapezoid, but placed entirely behind the mast).

H

HALYARD: a rope used to hoist a sail.

HOIST: a device made up of pulleys and rope intended to ease the effort in raising a sail or a heavy object.

I

INLET FITTING (of a pulley): the part of the pulley that contains the sheave.

L

LUGGER: a small coasting vessel with sails that can glide in the deepest of estuaries and bays to load or unload cargo.

M

MAKE FAST, TO: to stop a rope or other object from moving; to secure something.

MARLINESPIKE: a pointed metal tool with a hollow core that one slips between the strands of a rope to separate them when making a splice.

MOORING: the act of anchoring, or the place where boats are anchored.

MOORING POST: a vertical piece of wood or metal on the deck of a vessel to which the anchor line or mooring line can be attached.

P

PENNANT: a tapering flag, usually triangular, used for signaling.

R

REEF: the part of the sail bordered by eyelets, used to shorten the sail's surface (in strong winds or to slow down the boat).

REEF POINT: a thin rope used to keep the folds of the fabric in place when one shortens the sail.

ROBAND: a short piece of rope used in furling a sail.

S

SHEAVE: the rim of a pulley.

SHEET: a rope used to trim a sail.

STAND OFF, TO: to disembark or to remain offshore or apart from a boat.

STANDING END (of a rope): the part of the rope that is not used when one makes a knot.

SWIVEL (of a pulley): a fitting that allows the pulley to completely pivot upon itself.

T

TACK: the lower corner on the sail where it is attached to the deck of a boat.

TIGHTEN, TO: to apply great effort on something; a rope, an oar, the sailboat itself when one makes it bear a large area of sailcloth.

TOPMAN: a sailor who works on a large sailing vessel.

TOWPATH: a pathway made along a canal used by men or horses for the towing of boats.

W

WISHBONE MANROPE: rope serving to raise the rigging of a windsurf board.

WORKING END (of a rope): the part of the rope that one uses to make a knot, also called the running end.

INDEX